EXPRESSIONS
OF
Comfort

Helen Steiner Rice

BARBOUR
PUBLISHING

ISBN 978-1-59789-826-3

Devotional writing by Rebecca Currington in association with
Snapdragon Group ℠ Editorial Services.

The poetry of Helen Steiner Rice is published under a licensing agreement
with the Helen Steiner Rice Foundation.

Special thanks to Virginia Ruehlmann for her cooperation and assistance in the
development of this book.

Cover image © Aflo/Jupiter Images

Published by Barbour Publishing, Inc., P.O. Box 719, Uhrichsville, Ohio 44683

*Our mission is to publish and distribute inspirational products offering exceptional value
and biblical encouragement to the masses.*

ecpa Member of the
Evangelical Christian
Publishers Association

Printed in Malaysia.

Contents

God's Care

The LORD will keep you from all harm—he will watch over your life; the LORD will watch over your coming and going both now and forevermore.

PSALM 121:7–8

God loves you—*really, really* loves you! And like any loving parent, He has placed caring for you at the top of His list. When you run to Him, you will always find His arms open wide. You can be sure that He will always do what is best for you. You are not alone, dear friend; the great "I Am" is watching over you.

We are all God's children

and He loves us, every one.

He freely and completely forgives

all that we have done,

Asking only if we're ready

to follow where He leads,

Content that in His wisdom

He will answer all our needs.

Somebody cares and always will—

The world forgets, but God loves you still.

For God forgives until the end—

He is your faithful, loyal friend.

OUR FATHER IN HEAVEN ALWAYS

KNOWS WHAT IS BEST,

AND IF YOU TRUST IN HIS WISDOM,

YOUR LIFE WILL BE BLESSED.

Oh, God, look down on our cold hearts

and warm them with Your love,

And grant us Your forgiveness

which we're so unworthy of.

This is how God showed his love among us: He sent his one and only Son into the world that we might live through him.

1 JOHN 4:9

He's ever-present and always there

To take you in His tender care

And bind the wounds and mend the breaks

When all the world around forsakes.

When you're overwhelmed with fears

And all your hopes are drenched in tears,

Think not that life has been unfair

And given you too much to bear,

For God has chosen you because,

With all your weaknesses and flaws,

He feels that you are worthy of

The greatness of His wondrous love.

PLACE YOURSELF IN HIS LOVING CARE,

AND HE WILL GLADLY HELP YOU BEAR

WHATEVER LIES AHEAD OF YOU,

FOR THERE IS NOTHING GOD CAN'T DO.

I cannot dwell apart from You,

You would not ask or want me to,

For You have room within Your heart

To make each child of Yours a part

Of You and all Your love and care,

For You are love and Your love

should be everywhere.

There are many things in life

that we cannot understand,

But we must trust God's judgment

and be guided by His hand;

And all who have God's blessings

can rest safely in His care,

For He promises safe passage on

the wings of faith and prayer!

There's a lot of comfort in the thought

that sorrow, grief, and woe

Are sent into our lives sometimes

to help our souls to grow. . .

For through the depths of sorrow

comes understanding love,

And peace and truth and comfort

are sent from God above.

Just close your eyes and open your heart

And feel your worries and cares depart. . .

Yield yourself to the Father above

And let Him hold you secure in His love.

Put your hope in God, for I will yet
praise him, my Savior and my God.

PSALM 42:5–6

I come to You frightened
    and burdened with care,
So lonely and lost and
    so filled with despair,
And suddenly, Lord,
    I'm no longer afraid—
My burden is lighter and
    the dark shadows fade.
Oh, God, what a comfort
    to know that You care
And to know when I seek You,
    You'll always be there.

You're worried and troubled
    about everything,
Wondering and fearing
    what tomorrow will bring.
There is only one place
    and only one Friend
Who is never too busy,
    and you can always depend
On Him to be waiting,
    with arms open wide,
To hear all the troubles
    you came to confide.
For the heavenly Father
    will always be there
When you seek Him and find Him
    at the altar of prayer.

23

At times like these man is helpless. . .
It is only God who can speak the words that
    calm the sea,
Still the wind, and ease the pain. . .
So lean on Him and you will never walk alone.

God is no stranger in a faraway place—

He's as close as the wind

  that blows 'cross my face.

It's true I can't see the wind as it blows,

But I feel it around me,

  and my heart surely knows

That God's mighty hand

  can be felt everywhere,

For there's nothing on earth

  that is not in God's care.

arone...
some letter
made me wanted –
but was not force to
chappe it as he would.

God's Peace

And the peace of God, which transcends
all understanding, will guard your hearts
and your minds in Christ Jesus.

PHILIPPIANS 4:7

The whole world longs for peace—peace
of mind, peace of heart, peace in the
world around us. Where can you find it?
One place only—in the presence of our
Lord Jesus. His peace will surround you,
but it will also permeate you, bringing
comfort and calm. Even in the midst of
life's most powerful storms, you will be
unshaken.

27

After the clouds, the sunshine,

After the winter, the spring

After the shower, the rainbow—

For life is a changeable thing,

After the night, the morning

Bidding all darkness cease,

After life's cares and sorrows,

The comfort and sweetness of peace.

GOD BLESS YOU MOST ABUNDANTLY

WITH JOYS THAT NEVER CEASE,

THE JOY OF KNOWING THAT HE CAME

TO BRING THE WHOLE WORLD PEACE.

So kneel in prayer in His presence

and you'll find no need to speak.

For softly in quiet communion,

God grants you the peace that you seek.

God, be my resting place
    and my protection
In hours of trouble, defeat,
    and dejection.
May I never give way
    to self-pity and sorrow,
May I always be sure
    of a better tomorrow.
May I stand undaunted,
    come what may,
Secure in the knowledge
    I have only to pray
And ask my Creator and Father above
To keep me serene in His grace
    and His love.

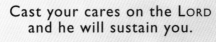

Cast your cares on the LORD
and he will sustain you.

PSALM 55:22

Do not be anxious, said our Lord,

Have peace from day to day—

The lilies neither toil nor spin,

Yet none are clothed as they.

The meadowlark with sweetest song

Fears not for bread or nest

Because he trusts our Father's love,

And God knows what is best.

I KNOW HE STILLED THE TEMPEST

AND CALMED THE ANGRY SEA,

AND I HUMBLY ASK IF IN HIS LOVE

HE'LL DO THE SAME FOR ME;

AND THEN I JUST KEEP QUIET

AND THINK ONLY THOUGHTS OF PEACE,

AND IF I ABIDE IN STILLNESS

MY RESTLESS MURMURINGS CEASE.

When your nervous network
    becomes a tangled mess,
Just close your eyes in silent prayer
    and ask the Lord to bless
Each thought that you are thinking,
    each decision you must make,
As well as every word you speak
    and every step you take—
For only by the grace of God
    can you gain self-control,
And only meditative thoughts
    can restore your peace of soul.

This brings you a million
good wishes and more
For the things you cannot
buy in a store—
Like faith to sustain you
in times of trial,
A joy-filled heart and a happy smile,
Contentment, inner peace, and love—
All priceless gifts from God above!

May peace and understanding
Give you strength and courage, too,
And may the hours and the days ahead
Hold a new hope for you;
For the sorrow that is yours today
Will pass away and then
You'll find the sun of happiness
Will shine for you again.

IF WE BUT HAD THE EYES TO SEE

GOD'S FACE IN EVERY CLOUD,

IF WE BUT HAD THE EARS TO HEAR

HIS VOICE ABOVE THE CROWD,

WE'D FIND THE PEACE WE'RE SEEKING,

THE KIND NO MAN AN GIVE—

THE PEACE THAT COMES FROM KNOWING

HE DIED SO WE MIGHT LIVE!

Take the Savior's loving hand

And do not try to understand—

Just let Him lead you where He will,

Through pastures green and waters still,

Though the way ahead seems steep,

Be not afraid for He will keep

tender watch through night and day,

And He will hear each prayer you pray.

"Come to me, all you who are weary
and burdened, and I will give you rest."

MATTHEW 11:28

When life becomes a problem
   much too great for us to bear,
Instead of trying to escape,
   let us withdraw in prayer—
For withdrawal means renewal
   if we withdraw to pray
And listen in the quietness
   to hear what God will say.

Silently the green leaves grow,

In silence falls the soft, white snow,

Silently the flowers bloom,

In silence sunshine fills a room—

Silently bright stars appear,

In silence velvet night draws near,

And silently God enters in

To free a troubled heart from sin.

God's Provision

Delight yourself in the LORD and he will
give you the desires of your heart.

PSALM 37:4

God is your provider, and He takes that
job seriously. He will not disappoint those
who trust in Him. In fact, He often answers before you can even ask. His provi-
sion may not come in the way you expect,
but it will always be what you really need.
He sees every situation from beginning to
end, and He provides accordingly. Find
comfort in your Father's unfailing care.

More than hearts can imagine

or minds comprehend,

God's bountiful gifts

are ours without end.

We ask for a cupful

when the vast sea is ours,

We pick a small rosebud

from a garden of flowers,

We reach for a sunbeam

but the sun still abides,

We draw one short breath

but there's air on all sides.

Whatever we ask for

    falls short of God's giving,

For His greatness exceeds

    every facet of living.

Just give Him a chance

    to open up His treasures,

And He'll fill your life

    with unfathomable pleasures.

Always God's ready and eager

and willing

To pour out His mercy,

completely fulfilling

All of man's needs for peace,

joy, and rest,

For God gives His children

whatever is best.

God has a storehouse

just filled to the brim

With all that man needs,

if we'll only ask Him.

Trouble is something
　　no one can escape—
Everyone has it in some form or shape.
But the wise man accepts
　　whatever God sends,
Willing to yield like
　　a storm-tossed tree bends,
Knowing that God
　　never made a mistake,
So whatever He sends
　　they are willing to take.
For the grandeur of life
　　is born of defeat,
And in overcoming
　　we make life complete.

In a myriad of miraculous ways

God shapes our lives and changes our days.

Beyond our will or even knowing

God keeps our spirits ever growing. . .

For lights and shadows, sun and rain,

Sadness and gladness, joy and pain

Combine to make our lives complete

And give us victory through defeat.

"Seek first his kingdom and his
righteousness, and all these things
will be given to you as well."

MATTHEW 6:33

THE LORD IS OUR SALVATION AND OUR

STRENGTH IN EVERY FIGHT,

OUR REDEEMER AND PROTECTOR,

OUR ETERNAL GUIDING LIGHT. . .

54

He has promised to sustain us,

He's our refuge from all harms,

And He holds us all securely

in His everlasting arms!

I am the Way, so just follow Me,

Though the way be rough

and you cannot see.

I am the Truth which all men seek,

So heed not false prophets

nor the words that they speak.

I am the Life and I hold the key

That opens the door to eternity.

And in this dark world, I am the Light

To a Promised Land

where there is no night.

No matter how big our dreams are

God's blessings are infinitely more,

For always God's giving is greater

Than what we are asking for.

While we cannot understand

  why things happen as they do,

The One who hangs the rainbow out

  has His own plans for you.

And may it comfort you to know

  that you are in His care,

And God is always with you,

  for God is everywhere.

"For I know the plans I have for you,"
declares the LORD, "plans to prosper
you and not to harm you, plans to
give you hope and a future."

JEREMIAH 29:11

Sometimes we come to life's crossroads
and view what we think is the end,
But God has a much wider vision,
and He knows it's only a bend—
The road will go on and get smoother,
and after we've stopped for a rest,
The path that lies hidden beyond us
is often the part that is best. . .
So rest and relax and grow stronger—
let go and let God share your load,
And have faith in a brighter tomorrow—
you've just come to a bend in the road.

Each day there are showers of blessings sent

from the Father above,

For God is a great, lavish giver,

and there is no end to His love. . .

And His grace is more than sufficient,

His mercy is boundless and deep,

And His infinite blessings are countless—

and all this we're given to keep.

Death of a Loved One

He will swallow up death forever.
The Sovereign LORD will wipe away the
tears from all faces; he will remove the
disgrace of his people from all the earth.

ISAIAH 25:8

Is your heart heavy, dear friend, and desperate with grief? God instructs us to comfort our hearts with His promise that this life is not the end. Those who are in Christ have been granted eternal life. It's only a matter of time until you are once again in the presence of your loved one. The separation stings, but it has no permanence. Place your hand in God's hand, and lay your head on His mighty shoulder. He understands.

WE ARE SO SAD WHEN THOSE WE LOVE

ARE CALLED TO LIVE IN THAT HOME ABOVE.

BUT WHY SHOULD WE GRIEVE

WHEN THEY SAY GOOD-BYE

AND GO TO DWELL IN A CLOUDLESS SKY?

FOR THEY HAVE BUT GONE

TO PREPARE THE WAY

AND WE'LL JOIN THEM AGAIN

SOME HAPPY DAY.

There is no death without a dawning,

No winter without a spring,

And beyond death's dark horizon

Our hearts once more will sing—

There will be no partings

And time is not counted by years.

Where there are no trials or troubles,

No worries, no cares, and no tears.

THROUGH THE DEPTHS OF SORROW

COMES EVERLASTING LOVE,

AND PEACE AND TRUTH AND COMFORT

ARE SENT FROM GOD ABOVE.

God has told us that nothing can sever

A life He created to live on forever.

So let God's promise soften our sorrow

And give us new strength

for a brighter tomorrow.

All who believe in God's

    mercy and grace

Will meet their loved ones face-to-face,

Where time is endless and joy unbroken

And only the words of

    God's love are spoken.

Like pilgrims we wander,
       until death takes our hand,
And we start on the journey
       to God's Promised Land—
A place where we'll find
       no suffering or tears,
Where time is not counted in days,
       months, or years—
And in that fair city
       that God has prepared
Are unending joys to be happily shared
With all of our loved ones
       who patiently wait
On death's other side to open the gate.

The LORD is my strength and my shield;
my heart trusts in him, and I am
helped. My heart leaps for joy and I
will give thanks to him in song.

PSALM 28:7

Death is only a stepping-stone

To a beautiful life we have never known,

A place where God promised man he would be

Eternally happy and safe and free.

When death's angel comes to call

God is so great and we're so small. . .

And there is nothing you need fear

For faith in God makes all things clear.

Today your heart is heavy

with sorrow and grief,

But as days turn to months

may you find sweet relief

In knowing your loved one

is not far away,

But is with you in spirit

every hour of the day.

Love like yours can never end

Because it is the perfect blend

Of joys and sorrows, smiles and tears,

That just grow stronger through the years.

So think of your loved one as living above,

No farther away than your undying love,

And now he is happy and free once more,

And he waits for you at eternity's door.

On the wings of death and sorrow
God sends new hope for tomorrow,
And in His mercy and His grace
He gives us strength to bravely face
The lonely days that stretch ahead
And know our loved one is not dead
But only sleeping and out of sight
Until we meet in that land
that is always bright.

Our dear ones pass on,

and we see them no more,

But we know they are waiting

on some other shore.

Death is just a natural thing

like the closing of a door,

As we start upon a journey

to a new and distant shore,

And none need make this journey

undirected or alone,

For God promised us safe passage to

this vast and great unknown. . .

$\mathcal{P}$ROCLAIMING TO

ALL DOUBTING MEN

THAT IN GOD ALL THINGS

LIVE AGAIN.

Flowers sleeping 'neath the snow,

Awakening when the spring winds blow;

Leafless trees so bare before,

Gowned in lacy green once more;

Hard, unyielding, frozen sod

So softly carpeted by God.

These miracles are all around

Within our sight and touch and sound,

As true and wonderful today

As when the stone was rolled away.

For God so loved the world that he gave his one and only Son, that whoever believes in him shall not perish but have eternal life.

JOHN 3:16

If Death should beckon me

with outstretched hand

And whisper softly of an unknown land,

I shall not be afraid to go,

I take Death's hand without a fear,

For He who safely brought me here

Will also take me safely back.

Man is but born to die and arise

For beyond this world in beauty there lies

The purpose of death which is but to gain

Life everlasting in God's great domain. . .

And no one need make this journey alone

For God has promised to take care of His own

Live for Me and die for Me.

And I, your God, will set you free!

Sickness

"I will restore you to health and heal your wounds," declares the LORD.

JEREMIAH 30:17

God created our bodies to run perfectly, but when sin entered the world they became frail—subject to sickness, fatigue, and injury. One day you will receive the body God intended for you, perfect and complete. Until then, God says to call on Him when your body is ailing.
Ask Him to heal you. Then receive His comfort. He will always be there for you.

*E*arthly pain is never too much

If He has bestowed His merciful touch

And if you look to Him and pray

He will help you through every day.

It makes me sad to think of you

Filled with pain and discomfort, too,

But I know there's nothing I can do

But talk to the Lord and pray for you.

Seed must be sown to
bring forth the grain,
And nothing is born
without suffering and pain,
And God never plows
in the soul of man
Without intention and purpose
and plan.

FOR ALL THINGS PASS,

AND THIS WILL, TOO,

AND WITH GOD'S HELP

YOU'LL COME SMILING THROUGH.

I wish I could wipe away every trace

Of pain and suffering from your face,

But He is great and we are small—

We just can't alter His will at all.

And none of us would want to try

For more and more, as days go by,

We know His plan for us is best

And He will give us peace and rest.

Though the way ahead seems steep

Be not afraid, for He will keep

Tender watch through night and day,

And He will hear each prayer you pray.

So place yourself in His loving care,

And He will gladly help you bear

Whatever lies ahead of you,

For there is nothing God can't do.

God can remove our uncertain fear

And replace our worry

    with healing cheer. . .

So close your eyes and open your heart,

And let God come in and freely impart

A brighter outlook and new courage, too,

As His spiritual sunshine smiles on you.

Blessings come in many guises

  that God alone in love devises.

And sickness which we dread so much

  can bring a very healing touch.

And through long hours of tribulation

  God gives us time for meditation,

And no sickness can be counted loss

  that teaches us to bear our cross.

Let us then approach the throne of grace with confidence, so that we may receive mercy and find grace to help us in our time of need.

HEBREWS 4:16

I wish I knew the right words to say

To take your troubles all away,

But at times like these we realize

That God who is both kind and wise,

Can do what none of us can do,

And that's to heal and comfort you.

I commend you to His care

And may He hear your smallest prayer

And grant returning health to you

As only He alone can do.

He is our Shepherd, our Father, our Guide,

And you're never alone

    with the Lord at your side.

So may the Great Physican attend you

And may His healing completely mend you.

IN SICKNESS OR HEALTH,

IN SUFFERING AND PAIN,

IN STORM-LADEN SKIES,

IN SUNSHINE AND RAIN,

GOD ALWAYS IS THERE

TO LIGHTEN YOUR WAY

AND LEAD YOU

    THROUGH DARKNESS

TO A MUCH BRIGHTER DAY.

Sickness and sorrow come to us all,
But through it we grow
    and learn to stand tall,
The more we endure
    with patience and grace,
The stronger we grow
    and the more we can face,
And the more we can face,
    the greater our love,
And with love in our hearts
    we are more conscious of
The pain and the sorrow
    in lives everywhere—
So it is through trouble
    that we learn to share.

"If you believe, you will receive whatever you ask for in prayer."

MATTHEW 21:22

Trials

Cast your cares on the LORD and
he will sustain you; he will never
let the righteous fall.

PSALM 55:22

Trials are a fact of life; they come to
each of us. But God is a cool oasis in the
midst of the desert. No matter what you
are going through, He is there by your
side ready to catch you if you should
fall. He knows all that you suffer, and He
offers you His comforting hand. "Come,
walk with Me," He says. "You can face
anything when we are walking through
it together."

When you're troubled and worried

   and sick at heart

And your plans are upset

   and your world falls apart,

Remember God's ready

   and waiting to share

The burden you find too heavy to bear.

So with faith, let go and let God

   lead the way

Into a brighter and less troubled day.

When the fires of life
burn deep in your heart
And the winds of destruction
seem to tear you apart,
Remember God loves you
and wants to protect you
So seek that small haven
and be guided by prayer
To that place of protection
within God's loving care.

Let us face the trouble

that is ours this present minute

And count on God to help us

and put His mercy in it.

And forget the past and future

and dwell wholly on today,

For God controls the future,

and He will direct our way.

*W*henever I am troubled

and lost in deep despair,

I bundle all my troubles up

and go to God in prayer.

It is life's difficulties and

the trial-times we go through

That make us strong in spirit

and endow us with the will

To surmount the insurmountable

and to climb the highest hill.

Seed must be sown to bring forth the grain,

And nothing is born without

suffering and pain,

And God never ploughs in the soul of man

Without intention and purpose and plan.

Do not be anxious about anything,
but in everything, by prayer and
petition, with thanksgiving, present
your requests to God.

PHILIPPIANS 4:6

When trouble comes, as it does to us all,

God is so great and we are so small—

But there is nothing that we need know

If we have faith that wherever we go

God will be waiting to help us bear

Our pain and sorrow,

    our suffering and care—

For no pain or suffering

    is ever too much

To yield itself to God's merciful touch.

God is the master builder,

His plans are perfect and true,

And when He sends you sorrow,

It's part of His plan for you. . .

For all things work together

To complete the master plan,

And God up in His heaven

Can see what's best for man.

While I am sure that You love me still

And I know in my heart

　　that You always will,

Somehow I feel that I cannot reach You,

And though I get down

　　on my knees and beseech You,

I cannot bring You closer to me,

And I feel adrift on life's raging sea. . .

But though I cannot feel Your hand

To lead me on to the Promised Land,

I still believe with all my being

Your hand is there beyond my seeing.

He has promised to sustain us,

He's our refuge from all harms,

And underneath this refuge,

Are the everlasting arms.

Cast your burden on Him,

Seek His counsel when distressed,

And go to Him for comfort

When you're lonely and oppressed—

For God is our encouragement

In troubles and in trials,

And in suffering and in sorrow

He will turn our tears to smiles.

Growing trees are strengthened when
they withstand the storm,
And the sharp cut of a chisel gives the
marble grace and form.
God never hurts us needlessly and He
never wastes our pain,
For every loss He sends to us is
followed by rich gain.
So whenever we are troubled and when
everything goes wrong,
It is just God working in us to
make our spirits strong.

There is always hope of tomorrow

to brighten the clouds of today. . .

There is always a corner for turning,

no matter how weary the way. . .

So just look ahead to tomorrow

and trust that you'll find waiting there

The sunlight that seemed to be hidden

by yesterday's cloud of despair.

But the Lord is faithful,
and he will strengthen and protect you.

2 THESSALONIANS 3:3

Soul Restoration

"Come to me, all you who are weary and
burdened, and I will give you rest."

MATTHEW 11:28

We all feel weary at times, ready to
give up. If that's how you feel, God wants
you to know that your own strength may
be small, but His is great. He is waiting,
eager to infuse you with new energy,
restore your vision, and help you carry
your burdens. You are not alone, dear
friend. Place all your burdens on Him
and receive rest for your soul.

Often we pause and wonder

When we kneel down to pray—

Can God really hear

The prayers that we say?

But if we keep praying

And talking to Him,

He'll brighten the soul

That was clouded and dim,

For though we feel helpless

And alone when we start,

Our prayer is the key

That opens the heart.

It's not money or gifts or material things,

But understanding and the joy it brings,

That can change this old world

    in wonderful ways

And put goodness and mercy

    back in our days.

Keep on believing, whatever betide you,

Knowing that God will be

with you to guide you. . .

And all that He promised

will be yours to receive

If you trust Him completely

and always believe.

Look ahead to tomorrow and trust that

you'll find waiting there

The sunlight that seemed to be hidden

by yesterday's clouds of despair.

THE FLOWER OF LOVE AND DEVOTION HAS

GUIDED ME ALL THROUGH MY LIFE;

SOFTENING MY GRIEF AND MY TROUBLE,

SHARING MY TOIL AND STRIFE.

While life's a mystery we can't understand,

The great Giver of life is holding our hand,

And safe in His care

    there is no need for seeing,

For in Him we live and move

    and have our being.

The LORD is my light and my salvation—
whom shall I fear?
The LORD is the stronghold of my life—
of whom shall I be afraid?

PSALM 27:1

127

God has given us the answers,

   which too often go unheeded,

But if we search His promises,

   we'll find everything that's needed

To lift our faltering spirits

   and renew our courage, too,

For there's absolutely nothing

   too much for God to do.

Thank You, God, for the beauty

around me everywhere

The gentle rain and glistening dew,

the sunshine and the air,

The joyous gift of feeling the soul's soft,

whispering voice,

That speaks to me from deep within,

and makes my heart rejoice.

For the Lord is our salvation

and our strength in every fight,

Our redeemer and protector,

our eternal guiding light.

Each time you smile you'll find it's true

Somebody, somewhere will

smile back at you,

And nothing on earth can

make life more worthwhile

Than the sunshine and warmth

of a beautiful smile.

There is nothing that we need know

If we have faith that wherever we go

God will be waiting to help us bear

Our pain and sorrow, our suffering and care.

The rainbow is God's promise

Of hope for you and me,

And though the clouds hang heavy

And the sun we cannot see,

We know above the dark clouds

That fill the stormy sky,

Hope's rainbow will come shining through

When the clouds have drifted by.

His goodness is unfailing,

His kindness knows no end,

For the Lord is a good shepherd

on whom you can depend.

He will guard and guide and keep you

in His loving, watchful care,

And when traveling in dark valleys,

your shepherd will be there.

To you, O LORD, I lift up my soul.

PSALM 25:1

Deliverance

The LORD is good, a refuge in times
of trouble. He cares for those
who trust in him.

NAHUM 1:7

Don't be frightened, dear friend. The
way before you may seem rocky, mys-
terious, and filled with danger; but you
are in the presence of someone much
greater than any dark shadow that may
cross your path. Even the fiercest enemy
is nothing in His eyes. You are safe with
Him. Replace your fear with the comfort
of His loving smile. Let Him show you
what His love can do.

WHEN LIFE SEEMS EMPTY

AND THERE'S NO PLACE TO GO,

WHEN YOUR HEART IS TROUBLED

AND YOUR SPIRITS ARE LOW,

THE BURDEN THAT SEEMS TOO HEAVY TO BEAR

GOD LIFTS AWAY ON THE WINGS OF PRAYER.

Sometimes the road of life seems long

    as we travel through the years

And, with a heart that's broken

    and eyes brimful of tears,

We falter in our weariness

    and sing beside the way,

But God leans down and whispers,

    "Child, there'll be another day."

Wish not for the easy way

    to win your heart's desire,

For the joy's in overcoming

    and withstanding flood and fire—

For to triumph over trouble

    and grow stronger with defeat

Is to win the kind of victory

    that will make your life complete.

THE ROAD WILL GROW MUCH SMOOTHER

AND MUCH EASIER TO FACE,

SO DO NOT BE DISHEARTENED—

THIS IS JUST A RESTING PLACE.

Another hill and sometimes a mountain

But just when you reach the peak—

Your weariness is lifted

And you find the peace you seek.

He will not let me go alone

Into the valley that's unknown.

Kings and kingdoms all pass away—

Nothing on earth endures.

But the love of God who sent His Son

Is forever and ever yours.

Teach us that it takes the showers
　　to make the flowers grow,
And only in the storms of life
　　when the winds of trouble blow
Can man, too, reach maturity
　　and grow in faith and grace,
And gain the strength and courage
　　to enable him to face
Sunny days as well as rain,
　　high peaks as well as low,
Knowing that the April showers
　　will make the May flowers grow.

And then at last may we accept

the sunshine and the shower,

Confident it takes them both

to make salvation ours.

This is how God showed his love
among us: He sent his one and only
Son into the world that we might
live through him.

1 JOHN 4:9

There are times when life overwhelms us

And our trials seem too many to bear—

It is then we should stop to remember

God is standing by, ready to share

The uncertain hours that confront us

And fill us with fear and despair.

For God in His goodness has promised

That the cross that He gives us to wear

Will never exceed our endurance

Or be more than our strength can bear.

Secure in a blessed assurance

We can smile as we face tomorrow,

For God holds the key to the future,

And no sorrow or care we need borrow.

When everything is pleasant and bright
And the things we do
    turn out just right,
We feel without question
    that God is real,
For when we are happy,
    how good we feel,
But when the tides turn
    and gone is the song
And misfortune comes
    and our plans go wrong,
It is when our senses are reeling
We realize clearly it's faith
    and not feeling,
For it takes great faith
    to patiently wait,
Believing God comes not too soon
    or too late.

What more can we ask of the Savior

Than to know we are never alone—

That His mercy and love are unfailing

And He makes all our problems His own.

My blessings are so many,

My troubles are so few,

How can I feel discouraged

When I know that I have You?

And I have the sweet assurance

That I'll never stand alone

If I but keep remembering

I am Yours and Yours alone.

Oh, Father, grant once more to men

A simple childlike faith again,

Forgetting color, race, and creed

And seeing only the heart's deep need. . .

For faith alone can save man's soul

And lead him to a higher goal,

For there's but one unfailing course—

We win by faith and not by force.

"Surely I am with you always,
to the very end of the age."

MATTHEW 28:20

Grace

It is by grace you have been saved,
through faith—and this not from
yourselves, it is the gift of God.

EPHESIANS 2:8

God's unmerited favor—that's what
grace is. He loves you, cares for you,
comforts and provides for you. . .even
though you don't deserve it. Don't waste
a moment thinking that you aren't good
enough to walk with God. He has made
you good enough by allowing His own
Holy Son to give His life in exchange for
yours. Linger long in God's grace.
It is His greatest gift.

*O*ur Father made the heavens,

The mountains and the hills,

The rivers and the oceans,

And the golden daffodils.

How wonderful to contemplate

And know that it is true

That He who planned the universe

Gave us our Savior, too.

The more we endure

 with patience and grace,

The stronger we grow

 and the more we can face,

And the more we can face,

 the greater our love,

And with love in our hearts

 we are more conscious of

The pain and the sorrow

 in lives everywhere—

So it is through trouble

 that we learn to share.

$\mathcal{L}$IFE IS CHANGE, BUT NEVER LOSS

FOR CHRIST PURCHASED OUR SALVATION

WHEN HE DIED UPON THE CROSS.

HIS GRACE IS ALL-SUFFICIENT

for both the young and old,

FOR THE LONELY AND THE TIMID,

for the brash and the bold.

162

If we place our lives in God's hands

And surrender completely

to His will and demands,

The darkness lifts

and the sun shines through,

And by His touch we are born anew.

No one has ever sought the Father

and found He was not there,

And no burden is too heavy

to be lightened by a prayer,

No problem is too intricate

and no sorrow that we face

Is too deep and devastating

to be softened by His grace.

"My grace is sufficient for you, for my power is made perfect in weakness."

2 CORINTHIANS 12:9

God asks for no credentials,

He accepts us with our flaws,

He is kind and understanding,

and He welcomes us because

We are His erring children

and He loves us every one,

And He freely and completely

forgives all that we have done.

We all have many things
  to be deeply thankful for,
But God's everlasting promise
  of life forevermore
Is a reason for thanksgiving
  every hour of the day,
As we walk toward eternal life
  along the King's highway.

Where can we find the Holy One?

Where can we see His Only Son?

The Wise men asked, and we're asking still,

Where can we find this Man of Goodwill?

Is He far away in some distant place,

Ruling unseen from His throne of grace?

EVERY DAY SOMEWHERE, SOMEPLACE,

WE SEE THE LIKENESS OF HIS FACE.

FOR WHO CAN WATCH A NEW DAY'S BIRTH

OR TOUCH THE WARM, LIFE-GIVING EARTH,

OR FEEL THE SOFTNESS OF THE BREEZE

OR LOOK AT SKIES THROUGH LACY TREES

AND SAY THEY'VE NEVER SEEN HIS FACE

OR LOOKED UPON HIS THRONE OF GRACE?

Realizing my helplessness,

I'm asking God if He will bless

The thoughts you think and all you do

So these dark hours you're passing through

Will lose their grave anxiety,

And only deep tranquillity

Will fill your mind and help impart

New strength and courage to your heart.

Tender little memories

of little things we've done

Make the very darkest day

a bright and happy one.

Tender little memories

of some word or deed

Give us strength and courage

when we are in need.

For each day at dawning we have but to pray

That all the mistakes that we made yesterday

Will be blotted out and forgiven by grace,

For God in His love will completely efface

All that is past, and He'll grant a new start

To all who are truly repentant at heart.

You believe in him and are filled with
an inexpressible and glorious joy.

1 PETER 1:8

God's Promises

Know therefore that the LORD your God
is God; he is the faithful God, keeping
his covenant of love to a thousand
generations of those who love him and
keep his commands.

DEUTERONOMY 7:9

A promise is of no value unless it is kept.
God keeps His promises—no matter how
great or small. He has instructed us to put
His promises to the test and in so doing
confirm His goodness and His faithful-
ness. He will never fail you, dear friend.
What He says He will do, He does. You
can anchor your life on that.

WHEN LIFE SEEMS EMPTY AND

THERE'S NO PLACE TO GO,

WHEN YOUR HEART IS TROUBLED

AND YOUR SPIRITS ARE LOW,

WHEN FRIENDS SEEM FEW

AND NOBODY CARES—

THERE IS ALWAYS GOD TO

HEAR YOUR PRAYERS.

The waking earth in springtime

reminds us it is true

That nothing really ever dies

that is not born anew. . .

So trust God's all-wise wisdom

and doubt the Father never,

For in His heavenly kingdom

there is nothing lost forever.

The love of God surrounds us

Like the air we breathe around us—

As near as a heartbeat,

As close as a prayer,

And whenever we need Him,

He'll always be there!

My blessings are so many,

my troubles are so few—

How can I be discouraged when

I know that I have You?

And I have the sweet assurance that

there's nothing I need fear

If I but keep remembering I am Yours

and You are near.

We've God's Easter promise,

    so let us seek a goal

That opens up new vistas

    for man's eternal soul. . .

For our strength and our security

    lie not in earthly things

But in Christ the Lord, who died for us

    and rose as King of kings.

There are many things in life

that we cannot understand,

But we must trust God's judgment

and be guided by His hand;

And all who have God's blessing

can rest safely in His care,

For He promises safe passage on

the wings of faith and prayer.

God's love endures forever—

    what a wonderful thing to know

When the tides of life run against you

    and your spirit is downcast and low.

God's kindness is ever around you,

    always ready to freely impart

Strength to your faltering spirit,

    cheer to your lonely heart.

God's presence is always beside you,

    as near as the reach of your hand.

You have but to tell Him your troubles—

there's nothing He won't understand.

And knowing God's love is unfailing,

and His mercy unending and great,

You have but to trust in His promise—

God comes not too soon or too late.

Now faith is being sure of what we hope
for and certain of what we do not see.

HEBREWS 11:1

Death is not sad. . .it's a time for elation,

A joyous transition. . .the soul's emigration

Into a place where the soul's safe and free

To live with God through eternity!

*W*hen God makes a promise,

It remains forever true,

For everything God promises

He unalterably will do.

When you're disillusioned

And every hope is blighted

Recall the promises of God

And your faith will be relighted,

Knowing there's one lasting promise

On which man can depend,

And that's the promise of salvation

And a life that has no end.

Secure in that blessed assurance,

    we can smile as we face tomorrow,

For God holds the key to the future,

    and no sorrow or care we need borrow.

We know that our Father

will richly provide

All that He promised

to those who believe,

And His kingdom is waiting

for us to receive.

My God will meet all your needs according to
his glorious riches in Christ Jesus.

PHILIPPIANS 4:19

America's beloved inspirational poet laureate, **Helen Steiner Rice**, has encouraged millions of people through her beautiful and uplifting verse. Born in Lorain, Ohio, in 1900, Helen was the daughter of a railroad man and an accomplished seamstress and began writing poetry at a young age.

In 1918, Helen began working for a public utilities company and eventually became one of the first female advertising managers and public speakers in the country. In January 1929, she married a wealthy banker named Franklin Rice, who later sank into depression during the Great Depression and eventually committed suicide. Helen later said that her suffering made her sensitive to the pain of others. Her sadness helped her to write some of her most uplifting verses.

Her work for a Cincinnati, Ohio, greeting card company eventually led to her nationwide popularity as a poet when her Christmas card poem "The Priceless Gift of Christmas," was first read on the Lawrence Welk Show. Soon Helen had produced several books of her poetry that were a source of inspiration to millions of readers.

Helen died in 1981, leaving a foundation in her name to offer assistance to the needy and the elderly. Now more than twenty-five years after her death, Helen's words still speak powerfully to the hearts of readers about love and comfort, faith and hope, peace and joy.